we are God's masterpiece

UNDERSTANDING
GOD'S PURPOSE AND PASSION
FOR YOUR LIFE

JOSEPH L. SCHLOSSER

Fresco – We are God's Masterpiece

Copyright © 2018 Joseph L. Schlosser. All rights reserved. No portion of this book may be reproduced mechanically, electronically, or by any other means, including photocopying, without written permission of the publisher. It is illegal to copy this book, post it to a website, or distribute it by any other means without permission from the publisher.

Excellent Press – Excellent Adventures Inc.
Atlanta, GA 30338
(404) 784-1008
joe@joeschlosser.net
joeschlosser.net

Unless otherwise indicated, all Scripture quotations are taken from The Holy Bible: New International Version. NIV. Copyright © 1973, 1978, 1984 by International Bible Society and New King James Version, Copyright © 1979, 1980, 1982 by Thomas Nelson, Inc. All rights reserved.

ISBN - 978-0-9889584-9-4

Introduction

Detail of Michelangelo's Sistine Chapel, painting in Rome, Italy

In 2014, after several hours of waiting on the Lord to reveal His purpose and calling on my life, I heard the words in my head, "*You are to do what I have called you to do, not what others are asking you to do.*" Then simply the word "fresco." After I got over the shock of "Did I really just hear that?" I began to pray into it.

From my graphics background, I knew fresco was a form of painting used by Michelangelo when he painted the Sistine Chapel at the Vatican in Rome, Italy. Regarding what I have been called to do, I was reminded of the time I was in Alaska and Isaiah 61 was prophesied over me –

The Spirit of the Sovereign LORD is on me,
 because the LORD has anointed me
  to proclaim good news to the poor.
He has sent me to bind up the brokenhearted,
  to proclaim freedom for the captives
  and release from darkness for the prisoners,[a]
² to proclaim the year of the LORD's favor
  and the day of vengeance of our God,
to comfort all who mourn,

³   and provide for those who grieve in Zion—
to bestow on them a crown of beauty
   instead of ashes,
the oil of joy
   instead of mourning,
and a garment of praise
   instead of a spirit of despair.
They will be called oaks of righteousness,
   a planting of the LORD
   for the display of his splendor.

As I began to research the process and technique known as fresco, the Lord began to reveal to me a parallel process of how He wants to infuse His purpose and perfect plan into our lives in a very similar way. Teaching this is how the good news will be proclaimed, captives will be freed, the brokenhearted will be mended and the prisoners released. Amen.

I invite you to copy and paste the link below, or scan the QR Code, to watch a short video explaining the fresco painting technique used by Michelangelo to better understand this comparison.

https://joeschlosser.net/fresco-technique/

The word *fresco* means fresh in Italian. I see it as a metaphor for these windows in our life when our sensitivity is really receptive to God's imprinting His purpose, His vision onto us. And the fresco process means fresh because it's painting on a fresh coat of plaster. The artist does several layers of preparation just getting ready for this very pure white coat that then receives an image to be imprinted on it, and then after painting the image and waiting for it to dry, seeing all the vibrant color exploding with vibrancy and lasting for thousands of years. That's why I really like this metaphor for starting a business, renewing an organization, or even something in terms of how you guide your life and career.

In fact, when asked, the Italian Master Artist Antonio DeVito said, **"The fresco technique is a perfect choice to illustrate the passion, creativity, but also perseverance and discipline one must have to start a business these days."**

The *fresco* process itself has 6 stages and I want you to walk through these stages with me. I'm going to use the metaphor of the fresco painting process and apply principles to understanding God's purpose and vision for your life - all of these principles are based directly from scripture. Then I'll share what I have learned through helping dozen of other ministries and businesses get started in what they were meant to do.

The first stage of the *fresco* process is the sketch. The sketch is the blueprint, the concept of what is going to be created. God usually gives us this sketch through the different stories and experiences from our life that reveal to us who we are meant to be. Those stories are hints at this masterpiece He is going to create in our lives.

After the sketch, the next step begins with the preparation of the surface. There are 3 layers of preparation in the *fresco* painting process. Each layer is more refined than the next layer, but each one has its own purpose that causes the whole process to stick together and last forever. For our *fresco*, the three foundational layers are faith, hope and love. Specifically what are the stories of faith, hope and love that have formed the foundation of your life?

Then, on top of that foundation comes a very pure smooth and receptive layer that is ready for the impression of God. That layer is applied bit-by-bit, section-by-section, because there is only so long for God's image to be impressed on us.

Once this layer is ready, the transfer of the image begins. In the *fresco* process they call this the transfer of the cartoon. It is the transfer of a piece of the larger sketch onto the wall.

After the sketch has been transferred to the surface, the next step is the application of the paint. Michelangelo only used 7 pigments of color to paint the fresco on the Sistine Chapel ceiling. I relate these 7 pigments of paint to the seven-fold spirit of Christ identified in Isaiah 11:1-3.

A shoot will come up from the stump of Jesse;
   from his roots a Branch will bear fruit.
² The **Spirit of the L**ORD will rest on him—
   the **Spirit of wisdom** and of **understanding**,
   the **Spirit of counsel** and of **might**,
   the **Spirit of the knowledge** and **fear of the L**ORD—
³ and he will delight in the fear of the LORD.

After the paint is applied, the *fresco* process then requires waiting for what was a messy process and for muddled colors to dry and for the brilliant, vibrant image to emerge. This is the period of time we need to rest in God. To be still and know He is God. Once the appropriate amount of time has passed, the vibrant colors emerge and you get an image, a representation of the artist's creation that lasts for generations and generations.

This is the *fresco* process.

****

The call of God the Father, opens a precious and critical moment in our lives. He is entrusting us with a picture of Himself He wants to reveal to the world, one that can only be expressed through us individually. In the same way Michelangelo painted a **fresco**, the image God the Father desires to create through us must be masterfully infused into the out-working of our call. But timing is also critical — every stroke of a God-given design must be completed before the plaster dries.

Each Chapter in this book is designed to walk you through the *fresco* process the Lord revealed to me.

Also, I invite you to join our Facebook group Launchpad Institute, and post questions to other members or our moderators. I trust you will find your great purpose in life as you engage the *fresco* process. Please let me know how I can be of assistance to you during your journey.

Blessings,

   Joseph L. Schlosser

Dedication

To my Lord and Saviour, Jesus Christ, who once told me I am to do what God, the Father, has called me to do, not what others are asking me to do. May I always have the courage to do that.

To my wife, Amy, for your love and support.

To my children, Alex and Hannah. May you embrace the masterpiece God has created you to be, running hard after your purpose and passion to find your true calling.

About the Author

Joe Schlosser's passion is people coming to know the love of Christ as they pursue what they are called to do. As an intense listener, great encourager, and servant leader, he has a desire to redefine the definition of ministry in an outside of the box way while still trusting the LORD in the process. He has worked with numerous national and local corporations, businesses, and nonprofits, applying his gifts in evangelism, strategic thinking, analysis, design, and creativity.

Joe is the founder and President of Excellent Adventures!, Inc., a small business and ministry marketing and communications firm. He also founded Kids Team, Inc., Excellent Marketing Group, Go Ahead Launch, LLC. and more recently the Launchpad Institute.

Joe graduated from Georgia Tech with an Architectural degree and worked in that industry for 14 years before launching out as an entrepreneur. He is married to Amy and has two beautiful children – Alex and Hannah. They now live in Atlanta, GA.

Remember in the dark
what you have seen in the light.

Jack Modesat

Contents

The Sketch 1
Foundations 13
Preparation 27
The Imprint 33
Painting Your Masterpiece 39
Convergence 47
Presentation 53

The Sketch

Gaining clarity about your unique purpose and calling

2 | The Sketch

The Sketch

Gaining clarity about your unique purpose and calling

The first step in the ***fresco*** process is the sketch. God gives us these little glimpses into the great masterpiece He is creating out of our life. He gives us glimpses of the projects He is giving us responsibility to build or take to the next level. In this section I want you to engage in a process of thinking about those things, going back and thinking about those stories - where has God shown you the sketch of your life? Where has God shown you the sketch of the project he has given you to accomplish?

You see these sketches in scripture all the time, and we really should have an expectation these kind of stories are woven throughout our lives as well. If you look at Joseph - God showed him in dreams, who he would become long before that ever became a reality. In the case of David, when he was a shepherd, he faced wild animals, then Goliath, thus showing what kind of king he would be. He was always this fearless king that engaged the enemy of the people of God and saying, "Man can't do this but God can."

Even Jesus, when he was 12 years old in the temple, was found in this exchange with the leaders of his day, with the rabbis, asking them questions and answering them in a way that had a different kind of authority behind it. That was exactly the kind of teacher he was going to be. The Living Word. When his parents showed up looking for him, they said, "How can you treat us this way?" He simply replied, "Did you not know I had to be about my Fathers business." As the Living Word, he always had to defy expectation and instead do exactly what the Father was doing - exactly what he was meant to do.

So let us too engage in this process - what are your stories? When did you feel the most alive? What are you meant to do?

****

4 | The Sketch

Gaining clarity about your vision or calling is really critical if you are going to succeed. All masterpieces begin with a basic sketch, often more than one. Key experiences in your life give hints to the masterpiece God has in mind. The key to the *fresco* approach is to put these experiences together to reveal God's thoughts for your life and work.

Knowing what you are meant to do with your life is more essential than what you have to do or what you want to do. I do believe God has a plan for all of us, and it is up to us to seek out what that is. I believe your true calling or purpose is revealed by **story**, or **peak experiences**, and **prophetic words** spoken over you, or through a **blessing** spoken by a parent or guardian.

For me, one of the most memorable peak experiences of my early life was hosting what I called the "*Fabulous February Fun Fest*". This was an annual weekend getaway, always centered on a long weekend in February where a friend and myself would organize a trip down to South Georgia to some land my family owned. My wife and I would invite all of our friends and have 10 + couples coming down to enjoy a crazy, fun weekend away. The 2,000-acre property was close to the beach and was also situated on a river so it was the best of all possible worlds. We would spend the weekend cooking, sitting around the fire, shooting guns, swimming and work on our testimonies :-). This weekend created in me a desire to serve others and see that they thoroughly enjoyed themselves. That has translated over to my desire to assisting entrepreneurs to be successful in their work, making sure they take time to enjoy everything they are doing.

As part of this exercise, you need to go back and think about those specific times in your life when you felt most alive or when someone spoke prophetically over your life and remember those experiences. Write them down so you can return to them over and over again.

Story and Peak Experiences

Peak Experience: a profound moment of love, understanding, happiness, or rapture, when a person feels more whole, alive, self-sufficient and yet a part of the world, and more aware of a virtue such as truth, justice, harmony, or goodness. In most cases, peak experiences involve a stat of "flow" in which personal and physical boundaries blur, the experience of time changes, and performance and ability align. Some may say this is when your "doing" and your "being" perfectly align with each other.

The Bible contains several "flash-backs" into the youth of important characters. These stories are included in the text specifically because they reveal something essential about identity and destiny. This implies this type of story, especially those containing peak experiences, as good indicators of our destiny as well.

> **Joseph:** A young boy who had dreams that saved a nation - Genesis 37
>
> **David:** A young hero shows the quality of his heart - 1 Samuel 17
>
> **Jesus:** A twelve-year-old takes the teachers of the law to school - Luke 2:41-52

Proclaimed Prophetically

Scripture is full of stories where God prophetically proclaimed a person's destiny to their parents or themselves at some point in their life through visions, prophetic words, and angelic visitations. The experience is so common in scripture; believers should entertain it as a possibility today.

Jeremiah: Before I formed you in the womb I knew you, before you were born I set you apart; I appointed you as a prophet to the nations. - Jeremiah 1:4-10

Who: Abraham, Joseph, Moses, Joshua, Sampson, Jacob, Esau, John the Baptist, Peter, and Paul

Given In A Blessing

In the Bible, parents have a special role proclaiming and confirming destiny in blessing their children. The following are examples given in the Bible:

Genesis 27:27-29 (NLT):

^{27} So Jacob went over and kissed him. And when Isaac caught the smell of his clothes, he was finally convinced, and he blessed his son. He said, "Ah! The smell of my son is like the smell of the outdoors, which the LORD has blessed!

^{28} "From the dew of heaven
  and the richness of the earth,
may God always give you abundant harvests of grain
  and bountiful new wine.
^{29} May many nations become your servants,
  and may they bow down to you.
May you be the master over your brothers,
  and may your mother's sons bow down to you.
All who curse you will be cursed,
  and all who bless you will be blessed."

Genesis 27:39-40 (NLT):

^{9} Finally, his father, Isaac, said to him,

"You will live away from the richness of the earth,
   and away from the dew of the heaven above.
40 You will live by your sword,
   and you will serve your brother.
But when you decide to break free,
   you will shake his yoke from your neck."

Genesis 49:1-28 (NLT):

Then Jacob called together all his sons and said, "Gather around me, and I will tell you what will happen to each of you in the days to come.

2 "Come and listen, you sons of Jacob;
   listen to Israel, your father.

3 "Reuben, you are my firstborn, my strength,
   the child of my vigorous youth.
   You are first in rank and first in power.
4 But you are as unruly as a flood,
   and you will be first no longer.
For you went to bed with my wife;
   you defiled my marriage couch.

5 "Simeon and Levi are two of a kind;
   their weapons are instruments of violence.
6 May I never join in their meetings;
   may I never be a party to their plans.
For in their anger they murdered men,
   and they crippled oxen just for sport.
7 A curse on their anger, for it is fierce;
   a curse on their wrath, for it is cruel.
I will scatter them among the descendants of Jacob;
   I will disperse them throughout Israel.

8 "Judah, your brothers will praise you.
   You will grasp your enemies by the neck.
   All your relatives will bow before you.

⁹ Judah, my son, is a young lion
  that has finished eating its prey.
Like a lion he crouches and lies down;
  like a lioness—who dares to rouse him?
¹⁰ The scepter will not depart from Judah,
  nor the ruler's staff from his descendants,[a]
until the coming of the one to whom it belongs,[b]
  the one whom all nations will honor.
¹¹ He ties his foal to a grapevine,
  the colt of his donkey to a choice vine.
He washes his clothes in wine,
  his robes in the blood of grapes.
¹² His eyes are darker than wine,
  and his teeth are whiter than milk.

¹³ "Zebulun will settle by the seashore
  and will be a harbor for ships;
  his borders will extend to Sidon.

¹⁴ "Issachar is a sturdy donkey,
  resting between two saddle packs.[c]
¹⁵ When he sees how good the countryside is
  and how pleasant the land,
he will bend his shoulder to the load
  and submit himself to hard labor.

¹⁶ "Dan will govern his people,
  like any other tribe in Israel.
¹⁷ Dan will be a snake beside the road,
  a poisonous viper along the path
that bites the horse's hooves
  so its rider is thrown off.
¹⁸ I trust in you for salvation, O Lord!

¹⁹ "Gad will be attacked by marauding bands,
  but he will attack them when they retreat.

²⁰ "Asher will dine on rich foods
   and produce food fit for kings.

²¹ "Naphtali is a doe set free
   that bears beautiful fawns.

²² "Joseph is the foal of a wild donkey,
   the foal of a wild donkey at a spring—
   one of the wild donkeys on the ridge.[d]
²³ Archers attacked him savagely;
   they shot at him and harassed him.
²⁴ But his bow remained taut,
   and his arms were strengthened
by the hands of the Mighty One of Jacob,
   by the Shepherd, the Rock of Israel.
²⁵ May the God of your father help you;
   may the Almighty bless you
with the blessings of the heavens above,
   and blessings of the watery depths below,
   and blessings of the breasts and womb.
²⁶ May the blessings of your father
   surpass the blessings of the ancient mountains,[e]
   reaching to the heights of the eternal hills.
May these blessings rest on the head of Joseph,
   who is a prince among his brothers.

²⁷ "Benjamin is a ravenous wolf,
   devouring his enemies in the morning
   and dividing his plunder in the evening."

²⁸ These are the twelve tribes of Israel, and this is what their father said as he told his sons good-bye. He blessed each one with an appropriate message.

Questions - The Sketch

1. What are the stories from your youth that hint at who you were uniquely made to be?

_____
_____
_____
_____
_____
_____
_____

2. Tell a story when you have felt most passionately and fully alive. Where were you and what were you doing?

_____
_____
_____
_____
_____
_____
_____

3. Can you think of a story told in your family, or one you experienced yourself, when your God-given destiny was proclaimed to you?

_____

_____

_____

_____

_____

_____

4. Has a parent, guardian, or person in authority over you ever proclaimed, confirmed, or blessed your God-given destiny? If yes, describe the experience.

_____

_____

_____

_____

_____

_____

_____

_____

Foundations

2

Building a solid foundation of virtues for your life and work

Foundations

Building a solid foundation of virtues for your life and work.

In the *fresco* painting process, the next step is to get the surface of the wall ready to receive this image created from the sketch. The first step of this process is called the foundation. The *fresco* process requires 3 layers of plaster to be applied that fill in the cracks and bond to the wall or surface providing a foundation for the rest of the painting. In our lives, Christ, He is our foundation, so we have to seek what it is in Christ that forms the bond helping keep everything grounded in place.

When you are in a business, career, or ministry living out God's masterpiece for your life, you have to have a foundation that will last through every storm and conflict that comes up. A foundation that keeps you on course with where God wants you to go. The Apostle Paul says, "These three remain: faith, hope, and love (1 Corinthians 13:13)." This is the foundation we find in Christ.

FAITH, HOPE, and LOVE

What are the stories of faith, hope and love in your life that will always be the guiding light, the anchor in the storm, the foundation on which you can build? By exploring these stories or experiences and keeping them in front of you, you can create with God something that builds His kingdom instead of something that crumbles or builds our own.

FAITH

When we think of these three foundations, the first one being faith, they are the rough undercoat. In the *fresco* painting process the first layer fills in the cracks on the wall. It is the most fibrous layer and really gets in and works its way into all the imperfections of the wall. All the rest of the layers will use this as their anchor point.

The writer of Hebrews defines faith as "the substance of things hoped for, the evidence of things not seen." Hebrews 11:1

Questions - Foundations (Faith)

1. Where did your story of faith begin? What has made your story of faith stronger?

_____

_____

_____

_____

_____

_____

2. Faith is an anchor. Tell a story that illustrates where your faith is anchored to hold firm in life's storms.

_____

_____

_____

_____

_____

_____

3. How will the next steps in your journey of life and work stretch and grow your faith?

_____

_____

_____

HOPE

This foundational virtue, hope, is the ability to stretch our vision towards something we cannot see. So my question to you is, "What is the hope that moves you forward?"

In the Old Testament, the story of Abraham is a great example of this. Abraham was told by God to pick up all of his household and belongings and move to a place yet to be determined. Abraham had faith that God would guide and direct him and he had hope for a future yet unseen.

This story talks about how faith and hope have a relationship to each other because Abraham had faith in the promises of God. He was able to then hope and stretch his vision out for a city whose founder and author was God alone.

Questions - Foundation (Hope)

1. In your life, what story or experience gives you hope for the future?

___

___

___

___

___

___

2. When you think ahead, what does the future look like? What picture are you trying to create?

_____

_____

_____

_____

_____

3. Christ is our hope. How does Jesus increase your hope for the future life and calling you've been given to carry out?

_____

_____

_____

_____

_____

4. As believers, we are told to be always ready to tell others about the hope we have. If asked today by a friend or neighbor, what would you say?

_____

_____

_____

_____

LOVE

The third layer of the *fresco* foundations is love. Paul says, "*Faith, hope, and love remain, but the greatest of these is love.*" (1 Corinthians 13:13)

John tells us "He who loves, knows God."

"*See what great love the Father has lavished on us, that we should be called children of God! And that is what we are! The reason the world does not know us is that it did not know him.*" 1 John 3:1 NIV

The layer of love is where we get in touch with the piece of the Fathers heart that is given to us. The question is, "What is your passion and in what way do you want to love the world?" What s this gift of the Fathers heart that he has given you to give away to others?

That is really what drives us on. God has only ever been in one business. The business of creating a family, building a nation, and raising a city. In all of this is the idea of a love that draws us into His identity. Gives us Him as our portion and inheritance and, in turn, we are His portion and His inheritance.

That co-possession and giving of each other back and forth is the only business of God. Whether you are starting a business, ministry, or career, whatever it is that's part of the masterpiece God is painting, there has to be a very stable foundation of the Fathers heart given to us that we can then give to others.

SPIRITUAL GIFTS

It has been said, "He who buries his talent is making a grave mistake." How true this statement is for so many of us. God has given each believer a spiritual gift that He wills us to use for His glory, but we oftentimes don't use it. We may deny that we actually have a gift or if we do acknowledge it, we may doubt its usefulness to glorify God, and then just bury it. But we must realize that God wants us to be involved with His work. He is so great that by His Holy Spirit He freely distributes gifts to all who are saved - and if He gives a free gift He not only wants us to use it but also expects us to.

The Bible says in Ephesians 4:7 "*But to each one of us grace was given according to the measure of Christ's gift.*" Also in I Corinthians 12:7 it says "*But to each one is given the manifestation of the Spirit for the common good.*" Then in verse 11 it states "*But one and the same Spirit works all these things, distributing to each one individually as He wills.*" So it is clear that each Christian has a spiritual gift. You may ask, "So what are they for? How do I use my gift (or gifts)? Does God really want to use me?

Let us first look at the question: Why do we have spiritual gifts at all? This will help us to determine the importance of the gifts.

In Acts 1:8, Jesus says, "*But you will receive power when the Holy Spirit has come upon you; and you shall be My witnesses both in Jerusalem, and in all Judaea and Samaria, and even to the remotest part of the earth.*" He is telling us the primary purpose of the gifts of the Spirit: to give the church power in order to preach Christ to the entire world. Paul says another purpose of the gifts is to equip the church for "building up the body of Christ" (Ephesians 4:12). He also reminds us in I Corinthians 14:12 that, "*So also you, since you are zealous of spiritual gifts, seek to abound for the edification of the church.*"

Therefore our goal should be to establish, build, and uplift the church with our gifts.

Still this doesn't quite answer the big question of why. Why build up the church?

Revelation 4:11 says, "*Worthy are you, our Lord and our God, to receive glory and honor and power; for You created all things, and because of Your will they existed, and were created.*" We are here to glorify God. To testify of His love, grace, and power. God wants to have a relationship with us through His son Jesus. But He also wants to have relationships with everyone else! That is why we, by His Spirit, need to do our part to help accomplish this. In John 15:8 Jesus says, "*My Father is glorified by this, that you bear much fruit, and so prove to be My disciples.*" By bearing much fruit, we glorify God, and we can only do this by abiding in Him and using our gifts to serve Him and bring others to Christ.

Why you?

You are needed in the body of Christ. If you are a Christian and are not serving in some way, we as a whole suffer from that. It's like missing a part of the body. You could probably live a normal life with just 9 out of 10 fingers. But you still wouldn't be able to do certain things as well as you would like. The truth is, the body of Christ has missing parts. They are attached but are missing in action. The church is called the "body of Christ" for a reason.

We are connected by our faith in Jesus Christ and sealed by the Holy Spirit. Being members of the body, we need to work together. In I Corinthians 12:12 it says, *"For even as the body is one and yet has many members, and all the members of the body, though they are many, are one body, so also is Christ."* And in verse 14, *"For the body is not one member, but many."*

Each of us is a specific body part. It sounds strange but it is a great analogy of the church. In verse 27 Paul affirms, *"Now you are Christ's body, and individually members of it."* If you read verses 13-27 you will see that Paul is telling of the importance of each member. He is also declaring that we need each member to function properly as a whole body. He says, in verse 26, *"And if one member suffers, all the members suffer with it; if one member is honored, all the members rejoice with it."*

You glorify God by getting involved.

God wants to use you! He has chosen you for the purpose of doing great things for Him. In Ephesians 2:10 it says, *"For we are His workmanship, created in Christ Jesus for good works, which God prepared beforehand so that we would walk in them."* God already has plans for you. He wants you to listen to His calling and make yourself available to serve. Not only that but, He expects you to use the gifts he has given you.

In Matthew 25:14-30 Jesus tells the parable of the talents. Though this is not specifically a parable on spiritual gifts, but on stewardship of the grace of God in our lives, spiritual gifts are called "grace gifts" and should be treated as such. A talent was a sum of money equal to about 15 years' wages. The master was leaving on a trip so he gave each of his three servants a different sum of money, according to their abilities, to invest with while he was gone. To one he gave five talents, to another two, and to the last servant one talent. When he returned, only two of the servants had used the money, each of them doubling the amount given to them. The third servant was afraid and had buried his one talent. When the master came to him to settle accounts the servant returned the original amount of money alone. The master was furious that his servant did not use it at all. He had the "wicked, lazy" servant thrown out and gave his talent to the one with ten talents. This illustration shows us that Christ wants us to use the gifts He has provided to us, not to bury them. In verse 29 Jesus says, *"For to everyone who has, more shall be given, and he will have an abundance; but from the one who does not have, even what he does have shall be taken away."*

So what's next?

The first step is to pray. Pray for God's guidance and ask Him to use you for His will. Ask Him to open your eyes and ears to His call on your life. He will undoubtedly put some direction or calling upon your heart. There are many existing places and ministries to serve in, or He may tell you to start a whole new one! Whatever God calls you to do, be confident He will provide a way for it.

Discover your gifts. You may already know what your spiritual gifts are. But, if you don't, or just want to clarify what they are, we have both an adult spiritual gifts test and a youth spiritual gifts test to help you find out. These tests do not guarantee what gifts you have, but they are helpful to get an idea. God may have given you gifts that you didn't think you could ever have. Or He may still transform some of your known talents into spiritual gifts. He will provide gifts for you to accomplish every goal He has for your life. Our gifts are to be developed as we mature. Philippians 1:6 says, *"For I am confident of this very thing, that He who began a good work in you will perfect it until the day of Christ Jesus."* Don't be afraid of what He will do with you. Step out in faith and let Him use you. The rewards will be great.

Find a church. If you are not attending a church, find one that is Spirit-filled, teaches the Bible and glorifies Christ. There are some helpful church searches available on our find a church page. Also, if you are not sure what specific ministry you are led to serve in, but you know what gifts you have, make sure that there is a place for you to serve there. God will use your service to strengthen your gifts and will work out the details in due time.

Be faithful, confident and humble. Faithfully serve in the small things and allow God to work in and through your life at His pace. Confidently apply your gifts whenever needed and humbly desire for Him to use you greatly.

Be a good steward of your gifts. God says if you are faithful with few things He will make you a steward over many things. I Peter 4:10 says, "As each one has received a special gift, employ it in serving one another as good stewards of the manifold grace of God." Use your gift or gifts at every opportunity to show the love, grace and power of God to others. This will produce fruit that remains and will glorify Him.

Most of all, Love. Use your gifts in love for the glory of God and the building up of His church. I Corinthians 13:13 says, "But now faith, hope, love, abide these three; but the greatest of these is love." Put on love in every situation and every time you serve, may God be the focus.

Questions - Foundations (Love)

The following questions are very important to the process. Open a word document and answer the questions below. Then email your answers to info@goaheadlaunch.com if you desire our comments.

1. What's your passion? How do you want to love those around you, those you're called to serve, and the world?

_____

_____

_____

_____

_____

_____

24 | Foundations

2. Have you been able to live out this passion? Tell us your best stories.

_____

_____

_____

_____

_____

_____

3. Love is contagious. Have you ever seen someone else's passion ignited when they encountered yours? If yes, in what way and how did that affect you?

_____

_____

_____

_____

_____

_____

Take a moment and reflect on the ***fresco*** process and what you have experienced so far. What is the Holy Spirit showing you about who God, the Father, says you are?

Notes:

Preparation

3

Establish a lifestyle of simultaneous peacefulness and readiness

Preparation

Establishing a lifestyle of simultaneous peacefulness and readiness.

Once the foundations have been laid in the ***fresco*** process, the next layer is one of preparation. This is the wet layer that will receive the painting. It is smooth, very white, and very pure. The intention is this layer stays wet while the image is transferred to the surface of the wall and then it's painted on so the pigment of the paint bonds with the surface very deeply.

To continue in our ***fresco*** process, this preparation of our life to be a masterpiece is what we refer to as Receptive Righteousness.

If we go all the way back to our belief of what will change the world and what we are meant to do, we were talking about how *in Christ* God has prepared works before hand to demonstrate His glory in the world that do the work of redemption and really changes things. The power to transform the world is *in Christ,* not in us. This is why receptive righteousness is essential.

We can be self-righteous and try to perform to a certain level, or you can be prohibitively righteous and refuse to do this or that. Receptive righteousness means you are laid down, surrendered, so the character and mind of Christ can be manifested in you, be born in you, and can sprout there. That mindset can lead to redemptive businesses. It can lead to organizations that give life, not take life. It can lead to careers, where not just one person is advancing in their potential, but the potential of one person catalyzing the potential of others. It's receptive righteousness. It is openness to receiving the righteousness of Christ. Think back to the scripture we have used talking about God's plan for redeeming the world and our part in that. It has always been said from a perspective of being *in Christ* - it's His faith, His righteousness, manifested in us that leads to the redemption of the world.

Whether our application of God's painting in our life is a business, a career, or a ministry, unless the righteousness of Christ is manifest in us we can't have any expectation the world will actually end up right. We have to ask ourselves, "Do we think more of us doing something or not doing something will set the world right?" No, it's the complete righteousness of Christ doing this. It is a person, not a to-do list. It is a person not a list of rules that sets the world right.

So this process of receptive righteousness is getting you ready, quieting yourself. Receiving God Himself through an outpouring of the Holy Spirit and everything that He wants to give you. That's receptive righteousness - laying down your life so he can do His work of raising you up again into what He wants you to be.

Questions - Preparation

1. Do you have a daily time of quiet reflection and prayer with the Lord? If yes, please indicate when you have your quiet time and how do you go about doing it?

_____

_____

_____

_____

_____

_____

2. What project or idea do you need to surrender and lay down before the Lord right now?

_____

_____

_____

_____

_____

3. Have you ever earnestly sought out the Holy Spirit to be poured

out upon you to be able to accomplish all that God wants you to achieve? If so, briefly describe what happened below. If not, in your own words, ask God the Father now to pour out His Holy Spirit upon you to accomplish the work He has called you to.

To understand more about who the person of the Holy Spirit is, I invite you to check out the free Biblically based teaching from PRMI at http://dunamisinstitute.org/video-courses.

Notes:

4

The Imprint

Grow your confidence in hearing God's voice and His leading

The Imprint

Grow your confidence in hearing God's voice and His leading.

After the preparation phase in the ***fresco*** painting process, the artist now transfers the sketch onto the surface of the wall. In our process, this is the Imprint stage where you are ready to receive the image of God. Everything is going to be done in a small manageable section. There is a portion of the sketch that will be blown up to scale and transferred into your life. This is what the imprint is all about.

Just like in the ***fresco*** process where the artist takes a portion of the whole image and transfers the lines into the wet plaster, God is giving you something right now that is part of the masterpiece for your life. It is really important to allow it to be impressed into you.

Whenever you receive an idea or vision of your future - write it down! Don't lose the idea! God's Word talks about the importance of doing this very thing.

Habakkuk 2:2-3 says,

"Write the vision
And make *it* plain on tablets,
That he may run who reads it.
³ For the vision *is* yet for an appointed time;
But at the end it will speak, and it will not lie.
Though it tarries, wait for it;
Because it will surely come,
It will not tarry."

Capture that moment by writing the vision down. Habakkuk talks about doing this. There is great wisdom in capturing this vision the Lord has provided for you.

There are two types of lines in the ***fresco*** process that I believe are instructions for us as well. The first is the solid line that is impressed into the plaster forming a solid break point. I believe this to be a firm boundary set by the Lord. Something He has given you in particular that He says, "It must be this."

Then there is the dotted line that implies a more general sense of where the color will be applied. This counsel of the Lord indicates you have the freedom to translate how it is might look in human form.

What I would like for you to do now is to sit down and start to look at what portion of the master sketch God is working on right now.

How does this apply to your business, organization or group you are working with right now? Start recording what you hear and recording how it relates to others. These become the boundaries and guidelines of what the Lord is about to paint.

Answer the question below, then find a quiet spot where you can settle down and hear from the Lord. Pray and ask God to show you this first part of His masterpiece planned for you. If you have already received a vision, now is the time to write it down so you don't lose it. Use the space below to capture this.

_____

_____

_____

_____

_____

_____

_____

_____

_____

_____

How Do You Know It's From God?

Sometimes we might get a great idea or incredible vision and wonder, is this really from the Lord or is it just me coming up with this? There is a very biblical way of knowing if the Lord is giving you a vision. Ask yourself these questions and if the answer is yes, then there is a good chance it is from the Lord. If you answer no to any of them, then be careful, as it may be something trying to get you off track and distracted.

1. Does it give glory to Jesus Christ?
2. Does it match up with God's Holy Scripture - the Bible?
3. Do other believers witness to it?
4. Will it bear fruit?

Painting Your Masterpiece

5

Working with God as you learn a daily spiritual rythym

Painting Your Masterpiece

Working with God as you learn a daily spiritual rhythm.

Now comes the part of the *fresco* process where God begins the painting process. In Isaiah 11:1-3 NIV it says out of the stump of Jesse, out of David's line, will come a shoot and that shoot will bear fruit. The way that shoot will bear fruit is through the seven-fold Spirit of God. We compare that seven-fold Spirit of God with the seven color pigments that Michelangelo used when he painted.

I interpret this seven-fold Spirit to be the complete character that rests on Jesus Christ.

> A shoot will come up from the stump of Jesse;
>   from his roots a Branch will bear fruit.
> ² The **Spirit of the LORD** will rest on him—
>   the Spirit of **wisdom** and of **understanding**,
>   the Spirit of **counsel** and of **might**,
>   the Spirit of the **knowledge** and **fear of the LORD**—
> ³ and he will delight in the fear of the LORD.
>
> Isaiah 11:1-3 NIV

I think it's a great way to form a daily rhythm and even larger rhythms that then translate into whatever you are doing, whether you are starting a business or simply doing what you've been doing for a while in your organization. It is translating the work of God, faithfully copying over what you are meant to do in this world. It is the match between heaven and earth.

When Isaiah talks about this seven-fold Spirit, he starts with the ***Spirit of the Lord.*** This is the only one that speaks of the Spirit as an identity. The rest are attributes. So this first Spirit is something that encapsulates all of the others. The first color we are painting with is the question "***What is the Lord giving me that is part of His dominion? What part of His responsibility does He want me to***

take on? When we ask the question in that spirit, He is faithful to answer.

The next two Spirits work together as all the rest of the Spirits will. It is the *Spirit of* **Wisdom** and **Understanding**. The next thing we want to do is paint with the colors of this sense of **"What wisdom is God giving me?"** and then the next question is, **"What understanding might I receive?"**

The word *understanding* means the creativity and comprehension the Lord is giving me. In this ***fresco*** process we want not only the wisdom and understanding He has given us, but also the wisdom and understanding He has placed in the relationships around us in our community.

From there comes action. As it says in Isaiah 11:2, the *Spirit of* **Counsel** and **Might** rested on Christ. In the same way counsel and might need to rest on us. **"What strength is God giving us to accomplish the work"** and **"What counsel is being giving us to show how to apply the strength?"**

Finally the last two colors correspond to the last two Spirits - the *Spirit of* **Knowledge** and the **Fear of God**. There is a sense that if we do the rest of this process faithfully we will realize this awe of Gods transcendence, His beauty. Something will rise up in us to praise him, worshipfully acknowledging how great He is. From that we will come to a greater knowledge of God.

These are the seven color pigments that God paints with. As you look at this phase of the ***fresco*** process, look at each of these in detail and talk about how they can be applied to your daily rhythm of living and even a larger rhythm for the things we are given to do. Write down and journal your thoughts.

Questions - Painting Your Masterpiece

1. Spend some time quieting yourself so you may pray to God and ask these questions. Acknowledge the Lord is the One in control and give praise to His name.

The first question should be "*What is the Lord giving me that is part of His dominion?*"

_____

_____

_____

_____

_____

_____

_____

2. The second question is *"What part of His responsibility does He want me to take on?"*

Share what you are hearing the Lord saying to you.

_____

_____

_____

_____

_____

_____

_____

3. The third question is ***"What wisdom is God giving me and what understanding might I receive?"***

_____
_____
_____
_____
_____
_____
_____

4. The fourth question is ***"What strength is God giving us to accomplish the work and how are we to apply this in our lives?"***

_____
_____
_____
_____
_____
_____
_____

5. Finally, ask yourself the final question, one that Jesus Himself asked His disciples *"**Who do you say God (I Am) is?**"*

_____

_____

_____

_____

_____

_____

_____

I encourage you to spend time on these questions. Go back to them often. The Lord says in His Word – ***Ask, and you shall receive***. Do this believing you will receive an answer. It may just surprise you.

Convergence

6

Experience more fruit being produced from your labor

Convergence

Experience more fruit being produced from your labor.

After painting a *fresco* there is a process we like to call Convergence. It is not a process of our activity but of our rest. In the Scriptures it talks about how one servant of God plants and another waters. In that reality there is a time of waiting from when the seed is planted and watered before you see anything sprout. You just have to wait before the sprouts come up; the plant grows and then produces fruit.

The same this is true for the *fresco* process. If you are painting this masterpiece, at first the paints seem very translucent and muddled. There is not a lot of colorful vibrancy and you don't know how they will all blend together. Often, As the Lord paints in our life and does His masterpiece; there are periods of doubt where we feel the same way. This is the time to rest in the promises of God. If we heard Him and we trust Him as a good Father to guard the word to make sure it will not return to Him void, then we can trust what He has painted in these seven spirits, what He has painted with the fullness of His character in our lives, will eventually become the picture we want to see.

The temptation is to see the messiness of it and act like the master is not in the room and we as the student rush in to fix it. Almost always when we do that we end up messing the masterpiece up. The more we try to fix it the worse we make it. We need to have instead an attitude of Sabbath, of being able to rest before God, seeing that he is completing His work. Just like with the fresco painting, the plaster will eventually dry and pull itself together, so will the colors of the fresco of our life pop into beautiful vibrant colors.

We will see the same thing in our lives. We will see fruit come out of our human imperfection. All things will work together for good for those who love God and are called according to his purpose. And it will pop. It will become this vibrant masterpiece. That is Convergence.

Questions - Convergence

1. Do you set-aside times of Sabbath and rest?

_____

_____

_____

2. What typically happens on those days or during those times of Sabbath rest?

_____

_____

_____

_____

_____

_____

_____

3. How would you describe your journey to date having gone through the *fresco* process?

_____

_____

_____

_____

_____

4. What do you believe God is calling you to do now?

Next Steps:

I trust the Father has revealed your passion and purpose to you through this *fresco* process. May The Lord bless you and go before you to prepare the way.

My heart beats with the *Barnabas principle*: When someone hears the Lord calling them to do something remarkable, amazing, or even impossible, they need **encouragers**, **equippers**, and **traveling companions** to come alongside. I offer resources and services to assist you to walk out your call in the special area God has gifted and launched you into. Feel free to contact me at any time if you have any questions.

Everything I do is focused on helping you and your organization **fully realize your calling**, *your* **faithful course of action**, *and the community you are meant to serve.*

I invite you to check out my blog and resources at joeshclosser.net and Launchpad-Institute.Thinkific.com.

Presentation

7

Invite others to witness God's work.

Presentation
Invite others to witness God's work.

The life of a Kingdom-seeker breaks all limitations and blesses others with God's own lavish love. Discover a humility-producing awe at the generosity of God in your life and work, and develop a contagious passion to share both the journey and the results.

Congratulations! You have successfully made it through the 6 steps of the *fresco* process and should now have a pretty good understanding of how God has created you and what your purpose in this life is. Now it's time to share what you have discovered with others!

Wrapping-Up The *fresco* Process

Now that the *fresco* process is complete, the last thing is to understand where this can take you. Do you have the obedience to be ready for the entire process, to step into each section and determine what God's doing right now. Let the work be added section-by-section, piece-by-piece. Understand it does not happen all at once, but rather as you participate with God, as He is doing the painting, the final product is something that can and will last for years and years.

One of the truths about God's business is it's never just for us. Christ came and heard no other thoughts than what the Father wanted to accomplish. That translated into love for us, love for humanity. In the same way, if we allow God to produce His masterpiece in us, our lives are not really ours. Our lives are for God and those that come after us. Those we invest in. Even in generations to come, ones we can't even see. It brings the promises of God not only to us, but also to those who are far off.

That's the kind of legacy we are to leave. The kind of life we want to live. The whole *fresco* process is targeting a sense of living in a spiritual way that brings the reality of God down to earth. It fulfills the prayer of Christ - *May the will of my Father in Heaven be done on Earth.*

That is what we are put on this earth for. Through this process it is our prayer that you'll be laying a foundation and painting with God in a way that will last a very long time, from generation to generation, bringing Heaven to Earth. I can't wait to see what you create!

Questions - Presentation

1. What has God revealed to you during this process?

_____
_____
_____
_____
_____
_____

2. What do you plan to do with this new knowledge about yourself and your purpose?

_____
_____
_____
_____
_____

Please allow me to pray the following scripture over you:

Whoever finds their life will lose it, and whoever loses their life for my (Jesus Christ) sake will find it.

Matthew 10:39 NIV

[16] I pray that out of his glorious riches He may strengthen you with power through His Spirit in your inner being, [17] so that Christ may dwell in your hearts through faith. And I pray that you, being rooted and established in love, [18] may have power, together with all the Lord's holy people, to grasp how wide and long and high and deep is the love of Christ, [19] and to know this love that surpasses knowledge—that you may be filled to the measure of all the fullness of God.

[20] Now to Him who is able to do immeasurably more than all we ask or imagine, according to His power that is at work within us, [21] to Him be glory in the church and in Christ Jesus throughout all generations, forever and ever! Amen.

Ephesians 3:16-21

Next Steps:

I trust the Father has revealed your passion and purpose to you through this *fresco* process. May The Lord bless you and go before you to prepare the way.

My heart beats with the *Barnabas principle*: When someone hears the Lord calling them to do something remarkable, amazing, or even impossible, they need **encouragers**, **equippers**, and **traveling companions** to come alongside. I offer resources and services to assist you to walk out your call in the special area God has gifted and launched you into. Feel free to contact me at any time if you have any questions. My contact information can be found at the beginning of this book under the copyright section.

Everything I do is focused on helping you and your organization ***fully realize your calling, your faithful course of action****, and the* ***community you are meant to serve.*** *Blessings be upon you.*

Other Resources

Make sure you check out these other resources at the Launchpad Institute – www.launchpad-institute.thinkific.com

The Pursuit of Freedom – Free Audio Course

With The Pursuit of Freedom, you understand your WHY, package your product, promote your product, and prosper with purpose. This course is all about how to get paid for your wisdom, knowledge, and experience.

Planning Your Best Year Ever – PDF Download EBook

This playbook walks you through how to set up and plan for your best year ever.

Your First Info Product – Online Course

Follow a proven info product system for generating real sales online from anywhere you have an Internet connection! Learn how to create an info product and sell it to the world.

Your First Sales Funnel – Online Course

Everything You Need To Set Up Your Online Sales Funnel.

Print On Demand Playbook – Online Course

Learn how to take what you know and turn it into a physical product such as a book or DVD.

[17 Goal Setting Strategies](#) – PDF Download EBook

Goals that are the most fun to set usually possess two golden qualities: They are attainable… yet stretch you out of your comfort zone. And they should always be in alignment with your most important values.

They also offer you one priceless benefit: Each goal advances you a step further towards attaining your dream lifestyle and business.

This workbook will walk you through 17 simple and fun strategies to create your most spectacular year ever!

[Weekly Social Media Planner](#) – PDF Download EBook

This simple, sought after Social Media Planner will help you plan out your social media marketing and posting on a weekly basis, freeing you up to do other things.

[JoeSchlosser.net](#)

A blog on all things Entrepreneurial and Starting a Business. Free resources and access to a thriving business community – CorEternal Business Group.

www.ingramcontent.com/pod-product-compliance
Lightning Source LLC
LaVergne TN
LVHW051157080426
835508LV00021B/2674